ALL-PRO FOOTBALL STARS 1977

JERRY BRONDFIELD

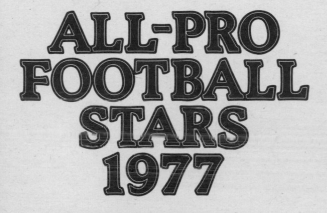

SCHOLASTIC BOOK SERVICES
New York Toronto London Auckland Sydney Tokyo

12 11 10 9 8 7 6 5 4 3 2 1   9   7 8 9/7 0 1 2/8

CONTENTS

The All-Pro Team of 1976

OFFENSE

WR: Drew Pearson, Dallas Cowboys
WR: Cliff Branch, Oakland Raiders
TE: Dave Casper, Oakland Raiders
 T: Ron Yary, Minnesota Vikings
 T: Dan Dierdorf, St. Louis Cardinals
 G: Joe DeLamielleure, Buffalo Bills
 G: John Hannah, New England Patriots
 C: Jim Langer, Miami Dolphins
 Q: Ken Stabler, Oakland Raiders
RB: O.J. Simpson, Buffalo Bills
RB: Walter Payton, Chicago Bears

DEFENSE

 E: Tommy Hart, San Francisco 49ers
 E: Jack Youngblood, Los Angeles Rams
 T: Jerry Sherk, Cleveland Browns
 T: Wally Chambers, Chicago Bears
LB: Jack Ham, Pittsburgh Steelers
LB: Robert Brazile, Houston Oilers
LB: Isiah Robertson, Los Angeles Rams
CB: Roger Wehrli, St. Louis Cardinals
CB: Monte Jackson, Los Angeles Rams
FS: Cliff Harris, Dallas Cowboys
SS: Ken Houston, Washington Redskins

Wide Receiver
DREW PEARSON
6-0, 185
DALLAS COWBOYS

Nobody seemed to want Drew Pearson when he finished up at Tulsa University in 1973. Tulsa had been run-oriented, and although Pearson was a regular, not too many passes were thrown his way. So, nobody drafted him. Dallas took him on as a free agent.

He didn't have great speed but, as a Cowboy coach said, "he could change direction like an antelope and shift gears into all kinds of change of pace. What he could do was leave a defender flat-footed."

After his second year, when he had more than 1,000 yards on 62 catches, the NFL honored him from then on with double coverage. Even so, he kept sharpening his sense of knowing where the defenders were, and kept on streaking into an open spot. With his great hands, he made all sorts of clutch plays.

This year, finally, there was no way he could be kept off the NFL All-Star team. QB Roger Staubach found him again and again as Pearson led the National Conference with 58 receptions for 806 yards and six touchdowns.

"I know where Drew is going to be," says Roger. "If the defense adjusts to cover that spot I still know he'll find another spot that's open. It makes a quarterback feel very good."

Wide Receiver
CLIFF BRANCH
5-11, 170
OAKLAND RAIDERS

When the fastest player in the NFL (under 4.3 for the 40-yard dash) has a great pair of hands, where do you play him? Right! You make him a wide receiver and let the enemy do most of the worrying. As an All-America at Colorado, Branch, who had run the 100 in 9.2, set an NCAA record for touchdowns on kick returns, with eight (two on kickoffs, six on punt returns). When the Raiders drafted him in the 4th round in 1972, he became a starter as a rookie.

With his dazzling speed and ability to get beyond the deep secondary, Branch immediately became a target for The Bomb. Defenders found it almost impossible to keep up with him. And once he got beyond them he was gone. The best defense against him was a prayer that the ball would not be on target—or that he would drop it, which he seldom did.

Last season as the Raiders swept to victory through the playoffs and in the Super Bowl, Branch caught 46 passes for a ton of territory—1,111 yards to be exact. His 12 touchdowns led the NFL, and his 24.2 yards per average gain was second only to the 25.9 mark by the Baltimore Colts' Roger Carr.

But Branch just doesn't depend on his speed. He can run short down-and-out patterns and can cut on a dime to leave a defender flat-footed.

Tight End
DAVE CASPER
6-4, 230
OAKLAND RAIDERS

The trouble with Dave Casper is that he doesn't look spectacular, even while he's doing an amazing job with the Raiders. But finally, this year, the former Notre Dame All-America convinced the critics that he's as good as the results he turns in.

"There's just no one better at all phases of his job," says Raider coach John Madden. "If he's just called upon to block, he explodes out of there and knocks his man right out of the play. If the assignment calls for him to block his man first, and then run his pass route, he does it, bang-bang. He hits, releases off his man, and next thing you know he's slipping into the seams of the zone coverage. He gets open as slick as any tight end I've seen."

There's one other thing. Or two. Casper has great hands for the ball. And once he tucks it away he's like a bull elephant. The secondary has to converge on him mighty fast, because it usually takes two to bring him down.

He doesn't have great speed, but he doesn't waste his moves. He knows where he's going at all times and when he and the ball arrive there together, the Raider drive is another 10 or 15 yards closer to the goal line. His 53 catches for 555 yards and 10 touchdowns gave him the best all-around stats for the year among tight ends.

Offensive Tackle
RON YARY
6-5, 255
MINNESOTA VIKINGS

You can count on the fingers of one hand the names of linemen who have made All-Pro six straight years. Now, add the name of the Vikes' Ron Yary. In Yary's case it was predictable. As an All-America tackle at Southern Cal, Yary won the Outland Trophy as the nation's best interior lineman. When the Minnesota Vikings made him the first draft pick in 1968, he was the first interior lineman to be drafted first in the NFL in 20 years. In two years he was a starter—and in 1971 became All-Pro.

"To really appreciate Yary," says a teammate, "you have to see him on film. He's amazing. He destroys people. I've seen him not only clean out the defensive end but take a couple of linebackers with him."

Another pro coach says: "With his strength, balance, and ability to recover quickly, it's impossible to run over him. It's suicide to try to charge straight into him. He fights you off and makes his block anyway."

Fran Tarkenton, the Vikings' quarterback, is another who appreciates Ron Yary. Few defenders get to the Viking signal caller on Yary's side of the line. (Unless you're an Oakland Raider, right?) Yary is also quick enough and smart enough to provide pass protection even when Fran does his famous scrambling act.

"Ron has great confidence," says John Michels, his line coach. "During a critical situation we may be talking about what we'll do on the next series. Ron just says: "Tell me where you want me to move my guy and I'll move him. Sideways, forward, backward, or into the stands."

Offensive Tackle
DAN DIERDORF
6-2, 280
ST. LOUIS CARDINALS

Do you need just one yard for a first down to keep your drive going? Simple. Just call the play over Dan Dierdorf's tackle position and you're on your way. When that situation rises for the St. Louis Cardinals, enemy defenses brace for Big Danny's charge. More often than not it doesn't do them much good.

It has been happening for several years. Finally, two years ago, the experts sat up and said: "Hey, it's time this guy was All-Pro!" So now Dierdorf has made it two straight years.

There are two things an offensive tackle must do to survive in the NFL, and Dierdorf does both. He's a great blocker on running plays and provides tight protection for his quarterback on passing plays.

Dierdorf, who was All-America at Michigan, is a big reason why Jim Hart, the Cardinals' great quarterback, is usually sacked fewer times by opposing linemen each season than any QB in the league. "It gives me more confidence," says Hart, "and more time to get my passes off, knowing that Dan is out there in front of me, keeping those big ends from getting to me."

Dierdorf is also a tough, durable player who has not missed a game with an injury in the last five years. He has excellent balance and is never out of position when he makes his block. The perfect offensive tackle.

Offensive Guard
JOE DeLAMIELLEURE
6-3, 245
BUFFALO BILLS

When some rookies come to the NFL, experts say: "He can't miss." But they do. When Joe DeLamielleure came up they said: "Not only is he going to make it, but he'll be All-Pro some day." This guy didn't disappoint *anybody*. This is his second straight year as the best in the business.

When the Bills' DeLamielleure was at Michigan State he majored in criminal justice. "I wish he'd have gone into crime busting instead of football," said an NFL linebacker. "When he comes out to lead interference you can just see that steely glint in his eye as he concentrates on getting his man. And he nearly always does."

A first-round draft choice in 1973, De-Lamielleure became an immediate starter for the Bills and made the All-Rookie team. It has taken him only two years to make the jump to All-Pro. But the way he leads interference and drops back for pass protection, everyone agreed he'd make it soon. He's also a ferocious straight-ahead blocker on running plays. "I love to run behind Joe," says O.J. Simpson, the Bills' super ballmover. "He's the kind of blocker a ballcarrier should remember in his will."

DeLamielleure three times made the All-Big Ten team in college, and topped it off with All-America in his senior year. Barring injury, he should be an All-Pro for many more seasons.

Joe has one more distinction going for him. He has one of the toughest names to spell in the entire NFL. If you don't believe it, take another look.

13

Offensive Guard
JOHN HANNAH
6-2, 265
NEW ENGLAND PATRIOTS

One of the surprises of the 1976 NFL season was the surge toward the top by the Patriots. Part of the surprise was a spirited new offense led by new quarterback Steve Grogan. But when you look for reasons behind the successful offense, most experts point to Big John Hannah.

A lot of the ground-gaining came over Hannah's position, where he was a tremendous straight-ahead blocker. But Hannah carried out his other chores equally well. He was super at pulling out to block on wide plays, and he gave Grogan excellent protection on passes.

Some people thought Hannah would have trouble in the pro's, after starring at Alabama. Because Alabama used a wishbone offense, Hannah did all his blocking straight ahead. What would happen when he had to do so many different things in the pro's? But 'Bama coach Bear Bryant said Hannah was the best lineman he'd ever had. "Don't worry about ol' Ham Hocks [Hannah's nick-name]," said Bryant. "He'll do it all."

Bryant was right, of course. Hannah became a starter as a rookie and made the All-Rookie team after being drafted on the first round in 1973. Except for one game in his first season, he's started every game for the Patriots since then. Look for more All-Pro years for ol' Ham Hocks.

Center
JIM LANGER
6-2, 253
MIAMI DOLPHINS

When a center snaps the ball to his
quarterback, it moves only about 20

inches. But an awful lot of timing and precision must go into it. The center and quarterback have to mesh perfectly or there'll be a fumble. Bob Griese, the Dolphin QB, never has to worry about Jim Langer.

Langer, a three-time repeater as All-Pro, was named South Dakota Sports Celebrity of the Year in 1972. South Dakota, a state with a very small population, doesn't have many nationally known sports figures, so when somebody from South Dakota earns the starting center job on the Miami Dolphins, he gets noticed at home.

Langer, a linebacker at South Dakota State, was a low draft choice with the Cleveland Browns in 1970. He was released on waivers early in the season and picked up by Miami. It was the best waiver pick-up the Dolphins ever made. By 1972 he was Miami's starting center.

Langer won the job by making a difficult switch from linebacker. He had to learn to snap the ball and make a quick, blocking charge. Many big linemen, no matter how strong and quick, can't adjust to the center's chores. It gets confusing when a defensive lineman across from him gets a free swat at him as the center snaps the ball. Often, too, the center has to snap and then get back quickly on pass protection.

Within two years after taking over as center for the Dolphins, Jim Langer was All-Pro.

Quarterback
KEN STABLER
6-3, 215
OAKLAND RAIDERS

Move over Johnny Unitas! Make way, Bart Starr, Joe Namath, Bob Griese, Roger Staubach, and Fran Tarkenton! A new superstar quarterback has arrived.

After nine Western Division titles in the AFC, the Raiders have finally made it to the top of the NFL with a Super Bowl victory. No more bitterness of final defeat. No more frustration. And Kenny (Snake) Stabler is the man who more than anyone else got them there.

A star at Alabama, Stabler was a number-two draft pick in 1963. Last season he was clearly one of the most exciting players in the NFL. His 66.7 percent passing completion is the highest since Bart Starr's a decade ago. He threw for 27 TDs, best in the NFL. He isn't afraid to run with the ball, and who will ever forget his bootleg run of three yards into the end zone to beat New England for the Super Bowl playoff spot.

A great field leader, Stabler's confidence spreads to his teammates. "When we're behind," says tackle Art Shell, "we never worry. We know The Snake can come up with the big play."

Twice in his career he has passed for more than 300 yards a game. Nineteen times he has thrown for more than 200 yards. How'd he get the name "Snake"? Once, during a high school game, he scored a TD on a play where he reversed his field at least four times, finally winding his way to a 70-yard score that must have traveled at least 150 before he reached the goal line.

19

Running Back
O.J. SIMPSON
6-1, 212
BUFFALO BILLS

Orenthal James Simpson is still the best
and most exciting runner in football. For
the third straight season, O.J. has to be
given the honor. His 1,503 yards rushing
led the NFL. And he did it even though he
reported late, out of shape, because of his
contract dispute with the club. It took him
at least three games before he was in top

gear. And with regular QB Joe Ferguson and Jim Braxton, the Bills' power fullback, sidelined most of the year with injuries, O.J. had to carry a bigger load than usual. Defenses were set to stop him—and still failed.

Everyone knew the former Southern Cal All-America was one of the greatest prospects ever to hit the NFL. Drafted No. 1 by the Buffalo Bills, he couldn't seem to get used to the cold northern weather. There also seemed to be smaller holes to blast through in pro lines than in college. His rookie season in 1969 found him gaining 697 yards rushing and 343 more on pass receptions.

The following year he suffered a knee injury and played only part of the season. In 1972, with his knee healed, he reached stardom, gaining the magic 1,000 yards for a season.

Everyone recalls Simpson's glory year of 1973 when he broke Jimmy Brown's all-time NFL career rushing mark of 1,863 yards. Not only did he break it, but in the final game of the season he set the "impossible" mark of a 2,000-yard season, winding up with 2,003.

Last year he broke still another of Jimmy Brown's marks when on Thanksgiving Day he rushed for 273 yards, his fifth career effort of more than 200 yards in a game. Would anyone bet there won't be a sixth?

Running Back
WALTER PAYTON
5-10, 211
CHICAGO BEARS

Walter Payton, the Bears' sensational second-year back, lost the NFL rushing crown to O.J. Simpson on the final day of the season, when he was injured in the first half and couldn't add to his yardage.

He may or may not have beaten out The Juice, anyway. No matter. Payton will be back again and again for the rushing honors. Everyone says he's bound to sew it up sooner or later. His 1,390 yards this past season are just a warm-up.

Payton, the 5-10, 211-pounder from Jackson State, had a good break-in year as a rookie in 1975. Not sensational, but he showed the moves that would get him to the top. And in 1976 those moves led the way for the Bears' surprising comeback from the several poor seasons they'd had. From now on, don't count the Bears out.

"It isn't just his speed," says one NFL coach, "it's his blinding quickness. A lot of guys can stop on a dime, but how many can be off again, full speed, on their first step?"

And a veteran NFL defensive back says: "He seems to come at you from all directions. I swear, he doesn't know himself which way he's going to cut."

His favorite maneuver looks like a broken play. He'll sweep right, see that he's cut off, and will stop and bolt all the way back to the left side. There won't be a blocker with him, but somehow he'll slice free for big yardage.

"The name of the game is confidence," says Payton. "I told them when I came up that I'd make it. Some people didn't listen because I wasn't all that big."

They're listening now, Walter.

Defensive End
TOMMY HART
6-4, 251
SAN FRANCISCO 49ERS

It seems that Tommy Hart has always
been at the top of his trade, but this was

the first year the critics recognized him. Never has an NFL player made All-Pro for the first time at such an advanced age. Hart has been a 49er for nine years. Always, he has been rock-steady, doing a super job, but getting little publicity. Other guys around the league—most of them not as good—were still getting the headlines.

Finally, there was no getting around it. Hart was so brilliant last season that he couldn't be put off any longer.

Hart was a linebacker at Morris Brown College in Atlanta, Ga., and was drafted as such by the 49ers. He weighed only 216 in college and was fast enough to run a 9.7 in the 100-yard dash. That would make him the fastest linebacker in the NFL.

Then he began building himself up, but losing very little of his speed. After a couple of years the San Francisco coaches thought his personality would make him a better defensive end than linebacker.

"Tommy's an 'attack' guy," said one coach. "At linebacker you have to back off sometimes, waiting to defend against the pass. You can't commit yourself immediately even on the run, until you see how it develops. As a defensive end he could always be on direct attack—and it turned out to be the best switch we ever made."

Quarterbacks and running backs around the league wished it weren't so.

Defensive End
JACK YOUNGBLOOD
6-2, 240
LOS ANGELES RAMS

If you make All-Pro, you're great. If you do it two years in a row, you're super. Three straight years and they'll begin measuring you for Hall of Fame some day. Who's to say Jack Youngblood won't make it?

"One of the rare sights in pro football," says an NFL coach, "is somebody putting a perfect one-on-one block on Youngblood. It's got to be 110 percent perfect or he's going to shuck it off and spoil the play."

Youngblood is a big reason why the Rams' defensive unit is always near the top of the NFL in rushing and scoring defense. Youngblood himself is the team leader in dumping the opposing quarterback.

The Rams had an idea he'd do things like that after he'd had an All-America year at the University of Florida in 1970.

In his first pro season, Youngblood was understudy to the Rams' great Deacon Jones. The following season Youngblood shared the left-end spot with Fred Dryer. When Jones retired and Dryer moved into the Deacon's spot, Youngblood was given a crack at the starting left-end position. With his strength and quick charge he gained instant stardom.

In 1973 he made second team All-NFL and was considered the Rams' outstanding defensive lineman. In 1974 he made All-Pro. Number four coming up?

Defensive Tackle
JERRY SHERK
6-4, 250
CLEVELAND BROWNS

"I'm just glad I never had to play against him," says Browns' coach Forrest Gregg. And Gregg should know how tough it'd be. He was a former All-Pro, himself, in his playing days.

But this is Sherk's first year as an All-Pro, even though he'd been named to the Pro Bowl team four times. "It's about time people recognized Jerry's real ability," says the Browns' defensive line coach, Dick Modzelewski. "He's the best defensive tackle in the NFL, even though some other guys have gotten more publicity and have played with teams with better records. Let me tell you what kind of player Sherk is—and how much effort he puts out. A couple of years ago he got knocked off the line of scrimmage, flat onto his back. But he got up, chased the play and ran down the ballcarrier 40 yards down the field. Never saw anything like it in my life."

A second-round draft pick in 1970 from Oklahoma State, Sherk was the Browns' only rookie starter that year. Cleveland coaches—and most other coaches in the NFL—are impressed not only by his strength and quickness, but by his alertness. He's always around the ball, and already has eight career fumble recoveries. He credits much of his quickness and agility to the fact that he was Big Eight heavyweight wrestling champion in college.

Defensive Tackle
WALLY CHAMBERS
6-6, 260
CHICAGO BEARS

"When Wally lays a hand on you," a veteran NFL back once said, "you feel it for a few days."

This Big Bad Bear has finally gotten the recognition he deserves. A first-round draft choice from Eastern Kentucky College in 1973, Chambers immediately sent up a signal by being named to the All-Rookie team, and was Rookie of the Year. As befits a guy who wears a ring through a pierced ear, he also predicted he'd be All-Pro some day.

In college he had led his team in tackles for three straight years, totaling 223. He brought that ferocious talent to the Bears. One of the fastest defensive tackles in the NFL, he also puts on a great pass rush. Opposing quarterbacks just hate to see his hulk coming at him, even if they get the ball away. They know that Wally can't be far behind.

The Bears, after being down for many years, are roaring on the comeback trail. Last year, with Walter Payton doing the ground-gaining and Wally Chambers anchoring the defense, they seemed to have gotten their act together again. Look for even better things this year.

Chambers has now started in 56 straight games and one of his goals is to make it at least an even 100.

Aside from quarterbacks and running backs, pro linebackers just might be football's more glamorous players. Certainly the competition for stardom among them is intense. Jack Ham is one who rises to the top each year. This is his fourth straight season as All-Pro. It's a habit he isn't expected to break soon.

One reason it was so tough to crack the Steeler defense was the best set of linebackers in the NFL. Jack Ham, Andy Russell, and Jack Lambert were the Terrific Trio which liked to hold its foes' gains in feet rather than yards.

Listen to a former All-Pro linebacker tell it like it is. Wayne Walker, who starred for the Detroit Lions and is now a TV sportscaster says: "Linebackers are usually among the most intelligent players on your team. They have to be, to make the many adjustments the position calls for. They have to defend against the run AND the pass and be able to smell out which it's going to be when so many plays start out the same way. Then they've got to have the speed and mental agility to adjust. And all the while, they're taking a beating from blockers who often crack them good while their attention is elsewhere."

That's Jack Ham. Ham was an All-America at Penn State in 1970. The Steelers made him their second draft pick in 1971 and he rewarded them by making the starting lineup as a rookie. He's not big as linebackers go—only 6-1 and 225 pounds—but he makes up for it in intelligence, quickness, and alertness.

Linebacker
ROBERT BRAZILE
6-4, 230
HOUSTON OILERS

When the Oilers made Robert Brazile, of Jackson State in Mississippi, their first draft choice in 1975, some experts said, "He'll make the pro's All-Rookie team, for sure." Others said, "He'll not only make All-Rookie, but in his second season he'll be All-Pro." Everybody was right.

Tremendously quick for his size, he also has great strength in his hands and arms, and has the ability to shuck off blockers who are trying to get him out of the play.

"But if it weren't for his strength and speed," says an opposing coach, "he could do it just as well with his smarts. I've never seen a linebacker come into the league and learn his trade so quickly. He plays like a five-year veteran, yet he has the enthusiasm of a youngster. It's obvious he loves what he's doing."

What he does so well is sack the quarterback, stack up the run, and defend slickly against the short pass. There just isn't any more that can be asked of a linebacker. If they ever invent a new demand, Bob Brazile will fill it.

Linebacker
ISIAH ROBERTSON
6-3, 225
LOS ANGELES RAMS

"Where'd he come from?" mumbled the
running back as he lay stunned on the

turf. Just an instant before, he'd been following his interference through a hole in
the Rams' defense. He was sure he'd seen
the Rams' linebacker, Isiah Robertson, get
blocked cleanly out of the play. But sud-
denly— POW!—the runner was hit by a
sledgehammer. The hammer was Isiah
Robertson.

It happens all the time. Robertson
NEVER is really out of the play. He hasn't
been since his college days at Southern
University in Texas, where he was an
All-America. As a linebacker, he'd also
intercepted 11 passes in his college
career, and the Rams liked that when they
drafted him.

Robertson made the Rams look good
when he won a starting job in his rookie
season and was named defensive rookie
of the year. Since then he's been named to
the Pro Bowl five straight years.

He's still up to his pass-stealing tricks.
Two years ago he had two of the longest
intercepts of the NFL season: one for 59
yards and one for 76. He's like a cat, with
instant reactions, sizing up the play in a
flash. If it's a run, there's Robertson clos-
ing the gap. If it's a pass, there he is flash-
ing backward or sprinting wide to knock it
down. He gets so close to a potential receiver he's almost illegal, according to
one NFL coach. Beating you by land or in
the air is what Isiah is all about.

Cornerback
ROGER WEHRLI
6-0, 190
ST. LOUIS CARDINALS

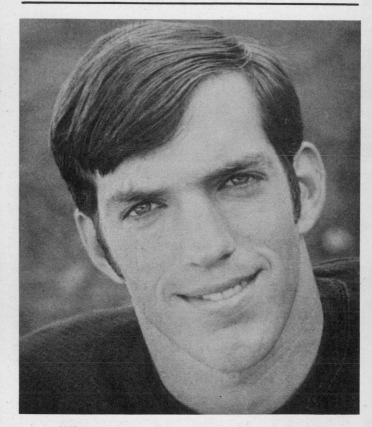

When you're describing Roger Wehrli,
the best word is C-O-N-S-I-S-T-E-N-C-Y.

Sometimes even the superstars don't seem to be putting it all together on a certain day, and wind up having a bad game. Wehrli just goes out and gives you the best he has (which is dazzling) and doesn't go above or below his level of real stardom.

Wehrli is another of those rarities in the NFL who starred as a rookie. A first-round draft choice back in 1969, the Missouri graduate impressed his pro coaches right away. At Missouri he had been an All-America defensive back as a senior; the year before he led the nation in punt-return yardage.

In 1970, a year after his rookie season with the Cardinals, Wehrli made All-Pro, and has since been up there with the best, except for 1972 when he was out with a knee injury.

"He doesn't look spectacular," says one veteran NFL observer, "but he has tremendous steadiness against both the pass and the run. You just can't count on Wehrli to make a mistake, mentally or physically. When he gets beat on a play it's only because the offensive guy has made an absolutely super, super play."

Often a choice for the Pro Bowl, Wehrli also was one of five NFL players to make a tour of U.S. military bases in Vietnam during the war. Just to keep the record straight, he pronounces his name WERE-lee.

Cornerback
MONTE JACKSON
5-11, 189
LOS ANGELES RAMS

When Monte Jackson was named to the NFL All-Rookie team in 1974, the question was asked: Can All-Pro be far behind?

Well, it took Jackson just two more seasons. There was no doubt that the Rams' second-round draft choice from San Diego State deserved the honor in 1976.

In two years at San Diego State, Jackson had intercepted nine passes. He returned them for a school record of 224 yards. The Rams were impressed. Jackson didn't start immediately, but fate took a hand. A regular Ram cornerback, Al Clark, was injured in the second game of Jackson's first season. Monte stepped in and sewed up the job permanently.

Jim Wagstaff, the Rams' defensive backfield coach, raves about his quick, tough star. "Monte is awfully tricky at the bump-and-run. He gives the receiver a good healthy crack as the receiver gets into his pass pattern, but Monte doesn't lose stride or momentum in staying with him downfield. He knocks an awful lot of receivers off balance."

Jackson isn't big, but he packs a wallop into his tackling, often jarring the ball loose from a receiver who has beaten him to the ball. Which doesn't happen very often. Jackson is a good leaper and can knock the ball away from much taller receivers. "It's all in the timing," says Wagstaff. "Monte knows exactly when to go up. He never commits himself too soon— or too late."

Free Safety
CLIFF HARRIS
6-1, 190
DALLAS COWBOYS

You'd have to say Cliff Harris made
All-Pro the hard way. In the first place,
he played for Ouachita (pronounced

42

WASH-e-taw) Baptist College in Arkadelphia, Ark. Not many football fans have heard of Ouachita Baptist and not many pro scouts know the airline schedules to Arkadelphia. So Harris had no pro teams searching him out. But he asked the Cowboys for a chance in 1970 and signed on as a free agent. From now on the Cowboys will keep Ouachita in mind.

Harris, a tremendous hitter, became an instant starter. But then he was called into military service and had to begin all over again when he came back. Same story. Regained his starting job immediately.

Harris is a master at psyching the receivers he has to cover. "I love to play a mental game with them," he says. "If you step in front of a receiver and make an interception he'll just be a little upset. But if you blast him and really spin his helmet around and ring his bell, he'll be looking for you from then on. He'll lose some of his concentration for the ball.

"Sometimes," he continues, "I even talk to them. I ask them, 'Is it worth it?' It sinks in and makes my job a bit easier."

No matter whether he plays a physical game or mental game, Harris can do it all. The only time he doesn't have football on his mind is in the summer when he works on getting his master's degree in environmental biology. He doesn't like things polluting the air. That includes footballs.

Strong Safety
KEN HOUSTON
6-3, 198
WASHINGTON REDSKINS

Some people are born to do certain things. Like a Rembrandt, to paint a picture. Like a Beethoven, to compose a great piece of music. Ken Houston, it seems, was born to knock down ballcarriers and intercept footballs.

Pass receivers or ballcarriers who break into the area patrolled by the Washington Redskins' strong safetyman know they are in for a rough greeting. It's the area guarded by All-Pro, three-time repeater Ken Houston.

A man who holds the NFL career record for touchdowns on pass interceptions (nine), and is a tough tackler, is a handy guy to have on your team.

When Houston played for Prairie View College in Texas, he was a linebacker at 6-3 and 198 pounds. Drafted by the Houston Oilers, he was moved to strong safety. The strong safety must be powerful enough to deal with 240-pound tight ends on passes. Although he was a ninth-round draft pick, he showed he was one of the best of the college crop.

He was a starter his first season with the Oilers. Within two years he was chosen for the Pro Bowl. Traded to Washington in 1973, he has had four great successive seasons.

"Ken has great instincts for the ball," says Redskin coach George Allen. "If a safetyman reacts just a split second too late, he can get beat for a touchdown. I just can't remember the last time that's happened to Houston."

Neither can enemy quarterbacks. They know they're taking a chance when they put the pigskin up deep, in Houston's area.

The All-Rookie Team of 1976

OFFENSE

WR: Steve Largent, Seattle Seahawks
WR: Sammie White, Minnesota Vikings
TE: David Hill, Detroit Lions
 T: Mark Koncar, Green Bay Packers
 T: Dennis Lick, Chicago Bears
 G: Tom Glassic, Denver Broncos
 G: Don Macek, San Diego Chargers
 C: Ralph Hill, New York Giants
 Q: Jim Zorn, Seattle Seahawks
RB: Clark Gaines, New York Jets
RB: Chuck Muncie, New Orleans Saints

DEFENSE

 E: Leroy Selmon, Tampa Bay Buccaneers
 E: Gary Burley, Cincinnati Bengals
 T: Steve Niehaus, Seattle Seahawks
 T: Mike Dawson, St. Louis Cardinals
LB: Harry Carson, New York Giants
LB: Greg Buttle, New York Jets
LB: Larry Gordon, Miami Dolphins
CB: Mario Clark, Buffalo Bills
CB: James Hunter, Detroit Lions
CB: Mike Haynes, New England Patriots
 S: Tim Fox, New England Patriots

Wide Receiver
STEVE LARGENT
5-11, 184
SEATTLE SEAHAWKS

It was the "steal of the century" when Seattle got Largent in a trade from Houston before the season started.... The Oilers thought he was too slow. "They simply misread his speed," says Jerry Rhome, Seahawk assistant coach. "He's a shade under 4.7 for the 40. And he has fantastic moves." At Tulsa University, where he was a brilliant student (8th in his class), Largent caught 136 passes for 2,385 yards and 32 TDs.... In his first Seahawk season he caught 54 for 420, great for a rookie—and with an expansion team.

Wide Receiver
SAMMIE WHITE
5-11, 189
MINNESOTA VIKINGS

Introducing Sammie White: Instant sensation ... Rookie of the Year .... The Vikes' number-two draft pick from Grambling College was a running back in college, but when the Minnesota coaches saw his slick moves and great hands they installed him at wide receiver.... Not overly fast but has magic moves and great ability to break free in his pass patterns.... Was a deadly threat on the long bomb all year .... Wound up with 51 receptions his first year, nifty stats for a newcomer.

Tight End
DAVID HILL
6-2, 220
DETROIT LIONS

The Lions knew he wasn't very big when they drafted him in the second round, out of Texas A & I, but they knew he was tough and confident.... Tight ends who only weigh 220 would normally have problems blocking 260-pound defensive linemen, but Hill had such quickness and such good blocking techniques that he made good immediately .... Nor did he let the Lions down when it came to catching the ball ....Averaged almost 20 yards per catch in college and came close to that in his first year as a pro.

Offensive Tackle
MARK KONCAR
6-4, 273
GREEN BAY PACKERS

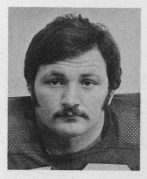

An All-America at Colorado, Koncar impressed Packer coaches with both physical and mental toughness .... In his very first season, veteran pro defensive players noted that he "exploded" off the ball in his straight-ahead drive blocking .... Also had good body control and nimble feet in quickly setting up for pass protection .... In college, built himself with weight lifting from 205 to 270 pounds .... Loves the outdoors, and spring ice-fishing in the Rockies is his favorite hobby.

Offensive Tackle
DENNIS LICK
6-3, 256
CHICAGO BEARS

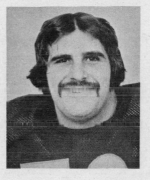

Once again the Bears are clawing their way to top ranking in NFL, after many years in the pits .... And one big reason is rookie tackle Dennis Lick, an All-America from Wisconsin .... He's a devastating blocker, and, paired with veteran Lionel Antoine at the other tackle, made it possible for the Bears' running game to click .... "I owe a lot to Denny," says Walter Payton, Chicago's All-Pro running back. "Any time I go to his hole I know he'll give me some daylight." Lots of it, in fact.

Offensive Guard
TOM GLASSIC
6-3, 254
DENVER BRONCOS

Denver's first-round draft pick was not only a starter as a freshman at North Carolina, but was also a dean's list student .... So, the Broncos knew they'd never have to explain something twice .... Denver's coaches knew in early drills that Glassic had excellent technique, and could not only blast straight ahead, but was quick enough to pull out and lead interference on sweeps .... The big defensive ends in the NFL didn't scare him at all as he escorted Bronco running backs downfield.

Offensive Guard
DON MACEK
6-3, 253
SAN DIEGO CHARGERS

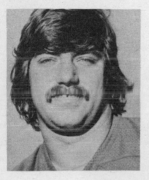

When the Charger scouts watched Macek in action his senior year at Boston College, they were a bit suspicious. Macek made things look too easy.... The scouts figured it was because B.C.'s competition wasn't that good.... But when they saw Macek blasting out the defense in two post-season All-Star games they knew Macek was for real.... They gave him a shot at starting in the pro's, and the second-round draft pick showed just as much strength and blocking ability as in college.

Center
RALPH HILL
6-1, 245
NEW YORK GIANTS

It took Ralph Hill longer than usual to reach "rookie" status, but once he did, he made the most of his chances. ... The former star from Florida A & M signed on with the Giants as a free agent. ... Three years ago, after college, he decided to go with Memphis in the new World Football League. ... When the WFL folded he asked the Giants for a chance. ... With the veteran Bob Hyland getting along in years, Hill shared time with him. He's the Giants' star center of the future.

Quarterback
JIM ZORN
6-2, 200
SEATTLE SEAHAWKS

You can't beat it as a success story. Although a Little All-America at Cal Poly, in Pomona, Calif., people paid little attention. . . . And though his stats at Poly were impressive, not many left-handed QBs get drafted. Zorn wasn't either. . . . He signed as a free agent in 1975 with Dallas and was cut. . . . A year later when Seattle became an expansion team they decided to try him—again as a free agent . . . ZOWIE! Who do you think became a starter and a star! Not bad stats for his first year: 208 completions and 12 TDs on 439 attempts.

The brightest hope in the Jets' somewhat dismal future, Gaines was their big surprise of the season. ... Didn't even make the pro draft, and came to the Jets as a free agent seeking a chance. ... Maybe the pro teams were scared off by his numerous injuries in college, where he starred for Wake Forest. ... With Joe Namath having a poor year and a passing game sub-par, Gaines' slashing running style and all-out effort provided the Jets with their best threat.

Running Back
CHUCK MUNCIE
6-2, 215
NEW ORLEANS SAINTS

The Saints knew what they were doing when they chose Muncie as the first running back to go in the 1976 draft. ...The big, All-America power back from the University of California showed in the pro's what he'd demonstrated in college: the ability to smash inside or sweep outside—and with amazing speed for a big runner. ... His 659 yards gained with a mediocre team in his rookie season predict a glittering future ... Muncie, who needs glasses when he plays, could never get used to contact lenses and is the only pro to wear full spectacles.

Defensive End
LEROY SELMON
6-2, 253
TAMPA BAY BUCCANEERS

An expansion team can't afford to gamble on its first-round draft choice — and the Bucs certainly didn't in picking Selmon, the Outland Award winner from Oklahoma, college football's best interior lineman of the previous season .... Selmon, one of three Sooner All-America brothers, was a tackle at Oklahoma, but because of his speed, the Bucs put him at defensive end .... Veteran NFL offensive tackles said he was among the toughest ends to block in the league .... "How can a rookie be that smart and tough?" growled one. He CAN be if he's Leroy Selmon.

Defensive End
GARY BURLEY
6-3, 255
CINCINNATI BENGALS

An All-America middle guard at Pitt in 1974, Burley was drafted as a poten tial offensive guard by the Bengals but was sidelined by an early season injury and never got to play.... Coming back last fall for his official rookie year, he was switched to defensive end because of his speed Smart at reading the enemy's running plays, he quickly became adept at containing the league's best ballcarriers.... Also put a determined pass rush on quarterbacks.

Defensive Tackle
STEVE NIEHAUS
6-5, 270
SEATTLE SEAHAWKS

The Seahawks, the other expansion club a year ago, were as fortunate as Tampa in their first pick .... Steve Niehaus was slated for super stardom ever since he started for Notre Dame in the very first game of his freshman year.... An instant star as a pro, the huge Niehaus had great upper body strength, which made him difficult to block, and he put great pressure on enemy quarterbacks with his fierce and fast pass rush .... He had knee operations two different years at Notre Dame but made a full recovery from both.

Defensive Tackle
MIKE DAWSON
6-4, 270
ST. LOUIS CARDINALS

The Cards' first-round draft choice from Arizona was voted outstanding lineman in the Western Athletic Conference .... What the Cardinal scouts liked about him was his fierce desire as he led his team in tackles for losses .... In pre-season drills as a pro, the big rookie showed that same flaming spirit .... Once installed as a starter, he battled the more experienced offensive linemen across from him and more than held his own .... Fast off the ball, he was a fine pass rusher.

Linebacker
HARRY CARSON
6-2, 228
NEW YORK GIANTS

After a dismal record most of the season, the Giants came back a bit in the last five games. One reason was Carson, who was logging a lot of playing time .... He started as a freshman at South Carolina State, starred for four years, and the Giants picked him in round four of the draft.... In his senior year at S.C. State he had 114 solo tackles and 30 sacks of the QB, possibly highest in the nation .... He didn't approach those stats in his rookie year with the Giants, but give him time!

Linebacker
GREG BUTTLE
6-2, 228
NEW YORK JETS

His coach at Penn State said Buttle was as good a linebacking prospect as any Penn Stater he's ever seen .... This included Jack Ham, the Steelers' All-Pro, which should make Buttle good enough .... The Jets, needing all the help they could get, got him right into action .... "He has natural instincts," opposing players soon said. "He reads offenses very well, and has the quick reaction and movements to get him to the ball, whether it's a run or pass." His father is an FBI agent.

Linebacker
LARRY GORDON
6-4, 230
MIAMI DOLPHINS

The first line-backer selected in the 1976 NFL draft, Gordon was labeled "can't-miss." An All-America at Arizona State, in his senior year he led the number-two-ranked Sun Devils on defense with an amazing 132 solo tackles. His athletic ability, plus speed and strength, brought him immediate playing time with the Dolphins, and soon was a regular....Was not often fooled by QB's faking and rarely was caught with a "blind-side" block .... A candidate for All-Pro some day.

Cornerback
MARIO CLARK
5-11, 185
BUFFALO BILLS

The Bills were frankly a bit surprised when Clark crashed the starting lineup in his rookie year .... Although he'd been a starter since his freshman season at Oregon and made All-Pacific Eight, the Bills figured it would take Mario a couple of seasons to learn the pro tricks .... But, a rugged tackler and a swift ballhawk who played the zone defenses as though he'd invented them, Clark got the job done in a hurry.

Cornerback
JAMES HUNTER
6-3, 195
DETROIT LIONS

Pro clubs are al-
ways embarrassed
when a first-round
draft choice falls on
his face. No way Jim
Hunter was going to
embarrass his boss-
es .... An All-Amer-
ica at Grambling
College, where he intercepted 26 passes
in his career, Hunter is one of the fastest
cornerbacks in pro football, unusual for a
man 6-3 .....But there was nothing gan-
gling about the big speedster .... A
beautifully coordinated athlete, he cov-
ered lots of ground and hit like a mad
rhinoceros in full charge.

Cornerback
MIKE HAYNES
6-2, 193
NEW ENGLAND PATRIOTS

Never has one team come up with two All-Rookie stars in the same back field. The Pats did it with Haynes and Tim Fox .... Haynes, an All-America at Arizona State, was the first defensive back chosen in the draft .... Led the nation in pass interceptions in college and will soon be noted for his thievery in the NFL .... Played opposition receivers as though he'd been studying their moves for years .... A hard hitter, Mike caused many a receiver to cough it up as soon as he hit him.

Safety
TIM FOX
5-11, 190
NEW ENGLAND PATRIOTS

The other half of the Patriots' sensational rookie secondary duo, Fox was an All-America at Ohio State . . . . Started four years for the Buckeyes, and in his senior year led  the Big Ten in punt returns . . . . His quickness and all-around athletic ability (a tumbler and high-jumper) make him an excellent pass defender, and his toughness makes him a strong and deadly tackler . . . . Seldom fooled by receivers in one-on-one situations . . . . Captain of his football, basketball, and track teams in high school.

1976 FINAL STANDINGS
AMERICAN FOOTBALL
CONFERENCE

EASTERN DIVISION

	W	L	T	Pct.	Pts.	OP
*Baltimore	11	3	0	.786	417	246
#New England	11	3	0	.786	376	236
Miami	6	8	0	.429	263	264
New York Jets	3	11	0	.214	169	383
Buffalo	2	12	0	.143	245	363

WESTERN DIVISION

	W	L	T	Pct.	Pts.	OP
*Oakland	13	1	0	.929	350	237
Denver	9	5	0	.643	315	206
San Diego	6	8	0	.429	248	285
Kansas City	5	9	0	.357	290	376
Tampa Bay	0	14	0	.000	125	412

CENTRAL DIVISION

	W	L	T	Pct.	Pts.	OP
*Pittsburgh	10	4	0	.714	342	138
Cincinnati	10	4	0	.714	335	210
Cleveland	9	5	0	.643	267	287
Houston	5	9	0	.357	222	273

*Division Winner
#Wild Card for Playoffs

AFC Playoffs
Oakland 24, New England 21;
Pittsburgh 40, Baltimore 14
AFC Championship
Oakland 24, Pittsburgh 7
Super Bowl XI
Oakland 32, Minnesota 14

and Previews for 1977 ...

EASTERN DIVISION

Baltimore Colts

Bert Jones...He'll crowd Ken Stabler for top quarterback honors in 1977.

QUARTERBACKING:	
RUNNING:	
RECEIVING:	
OFFENSIVE LINE:	
DEFENSE:	

New England Patriots

Tom Grogan...His quarterbacking may take Pats all the way to Super Bowl.

QUARTERBACKING:

RUNNING:

RECEIVING:

OFFENSIVE LINE:

DEFENSE:

Miami Dolphins

Fred Solomon...Developing into one of the trickiest receivers in NFL.

QUARTERBACKING:
RUNNING:
RECEIVING:
OFFENSIVE LINE:
DEFENSE:

New York Jets

Randy Rassmussen... Veteran guard is powerful blocker on Jet sweep.

QUARTERBACKING:
RUNNING:
RECEIVING:
OFFENSIVE LINE:
DEFENSE:

Buffalo Bills

Joe Ferguson...Buffalo QB is recovered from injuries, set for a banner season.

QUARTERBACKING:
RUNNING:
RECEIVING:
OFFENSIVE LINE:
DEFENSE:

WESTERN DIVISION

Oakland Raiders

Phil Villapiano...Fierce linebacker is just one of many Raider stars.

QUARTERBACKING:
RUNNING:
RECEIVING:
OFFENSIVE LINE:
DEFENSE:

Denver
Broncos

Rick Upchurch...Kills you
two ways: as top receiver and
punt returner.

QUARTERBACKING:
RUNNING:
RECEIVING:
OFFENSIVE LINE:
DEFENSE:

San Diego
Chargers

Charlie Joiner...Caught
passes for more than 1,000
yards last season.

QUARTERBACKING:
RUNNING:
RECEIVING:
OFFENSIVE LINE:
DEFENSE:

Kansas City Chiefs

MacArthur Lane... Has developed into one of NFL's best pass receivers.

QUARTERBACKING:	⬤ ⬤ ◖
RUNNING:	⬤ ⬤ ⬤
RECEIVING:	⬤ ⬤ ◖
OFFENSIVE LINE:	⬤ ⬤ ◖
DEFENSE:	⬤ ⬤ ⬤

Tampa Bay Buccaneers

Lou Carter.. .Led Tampa rushers last year, now has help from Ricky Bell.

QUARTERBACKING:	⬤
RUNNING:	⬤ ◖
RECEIVING:	⬤ ⬤
OFFENSIVE LINE:	⬤ ⬤
DEFENSE:	⬤ ◖

Pittsburgh Steelers

Rocky Bleier...His 1,000 yards last year finally made fans notice him.

QUARTERBACKING:
RUNNING:
RECEIVING:
OFFENSIVE LINE:
DEFENSE:

Cincinnati Bengals

Archie Griffin...Two-time Heisman winner is ready for big second year.

QUARTERBACKING:
RUNNING:
RECEIVING:
OFFENSIVE LINE:
DEFENSE:

75

Cleveland Browns

Greg Pruitt...His running will be the Browns' most consistent offensive threat.

QUARTERBACKING:	
RUNNING:	
RECEIVING:	
OFFENSIVE LINE:	
DEFENSE:	

Houston Oilers

Curly Culp...This tough defensive tackle is feared throughout the league.

QUARTERBACKING:
RUNNING:
RECEIVING:
OFFENSIVE LINE:
DEFENSE:

1976 FINAL STANDINGS
NATIONAL FOOTBALL
CONFERENCE

EASTERN DIVISION

	W	L	T	Pct.	Pts.	OP
*Dallas	11	3	0	.786	296	194
#Washington	10	4	0	.714	291	217
St. Louis	10	4	0	.714	309	267
Philadelphia	4	10	0	.286	165	286
N.Y. Giants	3	11	0	.214	170	250

WESTERN DIVISION

	W	L	T	Pot.	Pts.	OP
*Los Angeles	10	3	1	.750	351	190
San Francisco	8	6	0	.571	270	190
Atlanta	4	10	0	.286	172	312
New Orleans	4	10	0	.286	253	346
Seattle	2	12	0	.143	229	429

CENTRAL DIVISION

	W	L	T	Pct.	Pts.	OP
*Minnesota	11	2	1	.821	305	176
Chicago	7	7	0	.500	253	216
Detroit	6	8	0	.429	262	220
Green Bay	5	9	0	.357	218	299

*Division Champion
#Wild Card for Playoffs

NFC Playoffs
Minnesota 35, Washington 20;
Los Angeles 14, Dallas 12
NFC Championship
Minnesota 37, Los Angeles 7
Super Bowl XI
Oakland 32, Minnesota 14

and Previews for 1977 ...

EASTERN DIVISION

Dallas Cowboys

Roger Staubach...He'll be even more effective QB with Tony Dorsett running.

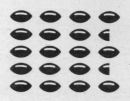

QUARTERBACKING:	⬤ ⬤ ⬤ ⬤
RUNNING:	⬤ ⬤ ⬤ ◖
RECEIVING:	⬤ ⬤ ⬤ ⬤
OFFENSIVE LINE:	⬤ ⬤ ⬤ ◖
DEFENSE:	⬤ ⬤ ⬤ ⬤

Washington Redskins

Bill Kilmer...An aging QB whose arm still makes the Redskins dangerous.

QUARTERBACKING:	⬤ ⬤ ⬤ ◖
RUNNING:	⬤ ⬤ ⬤
RECEIVING:	⬤ ⬤ ⬤
OFFENSIVE LINE:	⬤ ⬤ ⬤
DEFENSE:	⬤ ⬤ ⬤ ⬤

St. Louis Cardinals

Jim Otis...Hardnosed running gives balance to Jim Hart's quarterbacking.

QUARTERBACKING:
RUNNING:
RECEIVING:
OFFENSIVE LINE:
DEFENSE:

Philadelphia Eagles

Bill Bergey...Brilliant young linebacker is Eagles' best defensive player.

QUARTERBACKING:
RUNNING:
RECEIVING:
OFFENSIVE LINE:
DEFENSE:

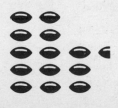

New York Giants

Larry Csonka...He'll have to have a big year if Giants are to come back.

QUARTERBACKING: 🏈🏈🏈
RUNNING: 🏈🏈🏈
RECEIVING: 🏈🏈🏈
OFFENSIVE LINE: 🏈🏈
DEFENSE: 🏈🏈🏈🏈◖

WESTERN DIVISION

Los Angeles Rams

Larry McCutcheon...His fancy running gives Rams strong Super Bowl hopes.

QUARTERBACKING: 🏈🏈🏈◖
RUNNING: 🏈🏈🏈🏈◖
RECEIVING: 🏈🏈🏈🏈◖
OFFENSIVE LINE: 🏈🏈🏈
DEFENSE: 🏈🏈🏈🏈◖

San Francisco 49ers

Gene Washington...A wide receiver with nifty hands and blazing speed.

QUARTERBACKING:
RUNNING:
RECEIVING:
OFFENSIVE LINE:
DEFENSE:

Atlanta Falcons

Haskell Stanback...A fine runner but needs a line to help him get loose.

QUARTERBACKING:
RUNNING:
RECEIVING:
OFFENSIVE LINE:
DEFENSE:

New Orleans Saints

Archie Manning...Without his strong arm, the Saints wouldn't have a prayer.

QUARTERBACKING:	🏈🏈
RUNNING:	🏈🏈🏈
RECEIVING:	🏈🏈
OFFENSIVE LINE:	🏈🏈
DEFENSE:	🏈🏈🏈

Seattle Seahawks

Norm Evans...Offensive tackle provides his QB with good protection.

QUARTERBACKING:	🏈🏈◖
RUNNING:	🏈🏈
RECEIVING:	🏈🏈
OFFENSIVE LINE:	🏈🏈◖
DEFENSE:	🏈🏈◖

CENTRAL DIVISION

Minnesota Vikings

Chuck Foreman...Vikes' great runner is truly one of NFL's superstars.

QUARTERBACKING:
RUNNING:
RECEIVING:
OFFENSIVE LINE:
DEFENSE:

Chicago Bears

Doug Buffone...Veteran linebacker anchors an improving Bear defense.

QUARTERBACKING:
RUNNING:
RECEIVING:
OFFENSIVE LINE:
DEFENSE:

Detroit Lions

Greg Landry...NFL's best running QB, gets lots of yardage on ground.

QUARTERBACKING: 🏈 🏈 🏈
RUNNING: 🏈 🏈 🏈
RECEIVING: 🏈 🏈 ◖
OFFENSIVE LINE: 🏈 🏈 🏈
DEFENSE: 🏈 🏈 🏈 ◖

Green Bay Packers

John Brockington...Packers are down, but a good year by Brock may help.

QUARTERBACKING: 🏈 🏈 ◖
RUNNING: 🏈 🏈
RECEIVING: 🏈 🏈 🏈
OFFENSIVE LINE: 🏈 🏈 🏈
DEFENSE: 🏈 🏈 🏈 ◖

How They're Picked
To Finish in 1977

NFC

EAST	WEST	CENTRAL
1. St. Louis	1. Los Angeles	1. Chicago
2. Dallas	2. San Francisco	2. Minnesota
3. New York Giants	3. New Orleans	3. Detroit
4. Washington	4. Atlanta	4. Green Bay
5. Philadelphia	5. Seattle	

AFC

EAST	WEST	CENTRAL
1. Baltimore	1. Oakland	1. Pittsburgh
2. New England	2. San Diego	2. Cincinnati
3. Miami	3. Denver	3. Cleveland
4. Buffalo	4. Kansas City	4. Houston
5. New York Jets	5. Tampa Bay	

Super Bowl XII
Oakland vs. Los Angeles

Best Bets for
Rookie-of-the-Year
Ricky Bell, Tampa Bay
Tony Dorsett, Dallas

1976 Records

SCORING

INDIVIDUAL CHAMPION
AFC: 109 Toni Linhart, Baltimore (kicker)
NFC: 97 Mark Moseley, Washington (kicker)

TOUCHDOWNS
AFC: 14 Franco Harris, Pittsburgh (14 Rushing)
NFC: 14 Chuck Foreman, Minnesota (13 Rushing; 1 Reception)

EXTRA POINTS
AFC: 49 Toni Linhart, Baltimore (50 Attempts)
NFC: 36 Tom Dempsey, Los Angeles (44 Attempts)

FIELD GOALS
AFC: 21 Jan Stenerud, Kansas City (38 Attempts)
NFC: 22 Mark Moseley, Washington (34 Attempts)

ONE GAME PERFORMANCE
AFC: 18 (3 TDs)
Reggie Rucker, Cleveland vs New York Jets, September 12; Roger Carr, Baltimore vs Cincinnati, September 19; Bob Chandler, Buffalo vs Kansas City, October 3; Morris Owens, Tampa Bay vs Miami, October 24; Rocky Bleier, Pittsburgh vs Tampa Bay, December 5; Freddie Solomon, Miami vs Buffalo, December 5; Ed Podolak, Kansas City vs Cleveland, December 12

NFC: 18 (3 TDs)
Delvin Williams, San Francisco (2) vs St. Louis, October 31 & vs Washington, November 7; Jean Fugett, Washington vs San Francisco, November 7; Walter Payton, Chicago vs Oakland, November 7; Lawrence McCutcheon, Los Angeles vs Atlanta, December 4; Sammie White, Minnesota vs Miami, December 11

TEAM LEADERS

AFC:

BALTIMORE 109 Toni Linhart; BUFFALO 60 Bob Chandler;
CINCINNATI 81 Chris Bahr; CLEVELAND 72 Don Cockroft; DENVER
81 Jim Turner; HOUSTON 72 Skip Butler; KANSAS CITY 90 Jan
Stenerud; MIAMI 77 Garo Yepremian; NEW ENGLAND 87 John
Smith; NEW YORK JETS 49 Pat Leahy; OAKLAND 72 Cliff Branch;
PITTSBURGH 84 Franco Harris; SAN DIEGO 42 Charlie Joiner;
TAMPA BAY 36 Morris Owens

NFC:

ATLANTA 50 Nick Mike-Mayer; CHICAGO 78 Walter Payton; DALLAS
88 Efren Herrera; DETROIT 49 Benny Ricardo; GREEN BAY 54
Chester Marcol; LOS ANGELES 87 Tom Dempsey; MINNESOTA 89
Fred Cox; NEW ORLEANS 70 Rich Szaro; NEW YORK GIANTS 44 Joe
Danelo; PHILADELPHIA 51 Horst Muhlmann; ST. LOUIS 93 Jim
Bakken; SAN FRANCISCO 74 Steve Mike-Mayer; SEATTLE 43 John
Leypoldt; WASHINGTON 97 Mark Moseley

TEAM CHAMPION

AFC: 417 Baltimore
NFC: 351 Los Angeles

TOP SCORERS — TOUCHDOWNS

	TDs Tot	TDs Rush	TDs Pass	TDs Misc	Pts Tot
Foreman, Chuck, Minn.	14	13	1	0	84
Harris, Franco, Pitt.	14	14	0	0	84
Grogan, Steve, N.E.	13	12	0	1	78
Payton, Walter, Chi.	13	13	0	0	78
Branch, Cliff, Oak.	12	0	12	0	72
Carr, Roger, Balt.	11	0	11	0	66
McCauley, Don, Balt.	11	9	2	0	66
McCutcheon, Lawrence, L.A. ..	11	9	2	0	66
Casper, Dave, Oak.	10	0	10	0	60
Chandler, Bob, Buff.	10	0	10	0	60
Johnson, Andy, N.E.	10	6	4	0	60
White, Sammie, Minn.	10	0	10	0	60

TOP SCORERS — KICKING

	XP Made	XP Att	FG Made	FG Att	Tot Pts
Linhart, Toni, Balt.	49	50	20	27	109
Moseley, Mark, Wash.	31	32	22	34	97
Bakken, Jim, St. L.	33	35	20	27	93
Stenerud, Jan, K.C.	27	33	21	38	90
Cox, Fred, Minn.	32	36	19	31	89
Herrera, Efren, Dall.	34	34	18	23	88
Dempsey, Tom, L.A.	36	44	17	26	87
Smith, John, N.E.	42	46	15	25	87
Gerela, Roy, Pitt.	40	43	14	26	82
Bahr, Chris, Cin.	39	42	14	27	81
Turner, Jim, Den.	36	39	15	21	81

AFC — INDIVIDUALS

	TD	TDR	TDP	TDM	XP	XPA	FG	FGA	PTS
Linhart, Toni, Balt. ...	0	0	0	0	49	50	20	27	109
Stenerud, Jan, K.C. ..	0	0	0	0	27	33	21	38	90
Smith, John, N.E. ...	0	0	0	0	42	46	15	25	87
Harris, Franco, Pitt. ..	14	14	0	0	0	0	0	0	84
Gerela, Roy, Pitt.	0	0	0	0	40	43	14	26	82
Bahr, Chris, Cin.	0	0	0	0	39	42	14	27	81
Turner, Jim, Den. ...	0	0	0	0	36	39	15	21	81
Grogan, Steve, N.E. ..	13	12	0	1	0	0	0	0	78
Yepremian, Garo, Mia.	0	0	0	0	29	31	16	23	77
Branch, Cliff, Oak. ...	12	0	12	0	0	0	0	0	72
Butler, Skip, Hou. ...	0	0	0	0	24	24	16	27	72
Cockroft, Don, Clev. .	0	0	0	0	27	30	15	28	72
Carr, Roger, Balt.	11	0	11	0	0	0	0	0	66
McCauley, Don, Balt. .	11	9	2	0	0	0	0	0	66
Casper, Dave, Oak. ..	10	0	10	0	0	0	0	0	60
Chandler, Bob, Buff. .	10	0	10	0	0	0	0	0	60

	TD	TDR	TDP	TDM	XP	XPA	FG	FGA	PTS
Johnson, Andy, N.E.	10	6	4	0	0	0	0	0	60
Mann, Errol, Det.—Oak.	0	0	0	0	35	37	8	21	59
Jakowenko, George, Buff.	0	0	0	0	21	24	12	17	57
Simpson, O.J., Buff.	9	8	1	0	0	0	0	0	54

NFC — INDIVIDUALS

	TD	TDR	TDP	TDM	XP	XPA	FG	FGA	PTS
Moseley, Mark, Wash. .	0	0	0	0	31	32	22	34	97
Bakken, Jim, St. L. ..	0	0	0	0	33	35	20	27	93
Cox, Fred, Minn.	0	0	0	0	32	36	19	31	89
Herrera, Efren, Da. ...	0	0	0	0	34	34	18	23	88
Dempsey, Tom, L.A. .	0	0	0	0	36	44	17	26	87
Foreman, Chuck, Minn.	14	13	1	0	0	0	0	0	84
Szaro, Rich, N.O.	0	0	0	0	25	29	18	23	79
Payton, Walter, Chi. ..	13	13	0	0	0	0	0	0	78
Mike-Mayer, Steve, S.F.	0	0	0	0	26	30	16	28	74
McCutcheon, Lawrence, L.A.	11	9	2	0	0	0	0	0	66
Thomas, Bob, Chi. ...	0	0	0	0	27	30	12	25	63
White, Sammie, Minn. .	10	0	10	0	0	0	0	0	60
Jones, Steve, St. L. ..	9	8	1	0	0	0	0	0	54
Marcol, Chester, G.B. .	0	0	0	0	24	27	10	19	54
Ricardo, Benny, Buff.—Det.	0	0	0	0	21	23	11	18	54
Thomas, Mike, Wash. .	9	5	4	0	0	0	0	0	54
Williams, Delvin, S.F.	9	7	2	0	0	0	0	0	54
Muhlmann, Horst, Phil.	0	0	0	0	18	19	11	16	51
Mike-Mayer, Nick, At. .	0	0	0	0	20	20	10	21	50
Galbreath, Tony, N.O. .	8	7	1	0	0	0	0	0	48

RUSHING

INDIVIDUAL CHAMPION
AFC: 1,503 (Yards) O.J. Simpson, Buffalo
NFC: 1,390 (Yards) Walter Payton, Chicago

AVERAGE
AFC: 5.6 (Yards) Don Calhoun, New England (721 Yards, 129 Attempts)
NFC: 4.9 (Yards) Delvin Williams, San Francisco (1,203 Yards, 248 Attempts)

TOUCHDOWNS
AFC: 14 Franco Harris, Pittsburgh
NFC: 13 Chuck Foreman, Minnesota, Walter Payton, Chicago

ATTEMPTS
AFC: 290 O.J. Simpson, Buffalo
NFC: 311 Walter Payton, Chicago

LONGEST
AFC: 77 (Yards) Archie Griffin, Cincinnati vs Houston, November 21 (TD)
NFC: 80 (Yards) Delvin Williams, San Francisco vs Washington, November 7 (TD)

ONE GAME PERFORMANCE
AFC: 273 (Yards, 29 Attempts) O.J. Simpson, Buffalo vs Detroit, November 25, a new NFL game record
NFC: 200 (Yards, 28 Attempts) Chuck Foreman, Minnesota vs Philadelphia, October 24

TEAM LEADERS
AFC:
BALTIMORE 1,200 Lydell Mitchell; BUFFALO 1,503 O.J.Simpson; CINCINNATI 671 Boobie Clark; CLEVELAND 1,000 Greg Pruitt; DENVER 1,008 Otis Armstrong; HOUSTON 684 Ronnie Coleman; KANSAS CITY 542 MacArthur Lane; MIAMI 797 Benny Malone; NEW ENGLAND 824 Sam Cunningham; NEW YORK JETS 724 Clark

Gaines; OAKLAND 1,012 Mark van Eeghen; PITTSBURGH 1,128
Franco Harris; SAN DIEGO 802 Ricky Young; TAMPA BAY 521 Louis
Carter

NFC:
ATLANTA 428 Bubba Bean; CHICAGO 1,390 Walter Payton; DALLAS
542 Doug Dennison; DETROIT 858 Dexter Bussey; GREEN BAY 435
Willard Harrell; LOS ANGELES 1,168 Lawrence McCutcheon;
MINNESOTA 1,155 Chuck Foreman; NEW ORLEANS 659 Chuck
Muncie; NEW YORK GIANTS 731 Doug Kotar; PHILADELPHIA 561
Mike Hogan; ST. LOUIS 891 Jim Otis; SAN FRANCISCO 1,203 Delvin
Williams; SEATTLE 537 Sherman Smith; WASHINGTON 1,101 Mike
Thomas

TEAM CHAMPION
AFC: 2,971 (Yards) Pittsburgh (653 Attempts; 4.5 Average)
NFC: 2,528 (Yards) Los Angeles (613 Attempts; 4.1 Average)

TOP TEN RUSHERS

	Att	Yards	Avg	Long	TDs
Simpson, O.J., Buff.	290	1503	5.2	t75	8
Payton, Walter, Chi.	311	1390	4.5	60	13
Williams, Delvin, S.F.	248	1203	4.9	t80	7
Mitchell, Lydell, Balt.	289	1200	4.2	43	5
McCutcheon, Lawrence, L.A. ..	291	1168	4.0	40	9
Foreman, Chuck, Minn.	278	1155	4.2	46	13
Harris, Franco, Pitt.	289	1128	3.9	30	14
Thomas, Mike, Wash.	254	1101	4.3	28	5
Bleier, Rocky, Pitt.	220	1036	4.7	28	5
van Eeghen, Mark, Oak.	233	1012	4.3	21	3

AFC — INDIVIDUALS

	Att	Yards	Avg	Long	TDs
Simpson, O.J., Buff.	290	1503	5.2	t75	8
Mitchell, Lydell, Balt.	289	1200	4.2	43	5
Harris, Franco, Pitt.	289	1128	3.9	30	14
Bleier, Rocky, Pitt.	220	1036	4.7	28	5
van Eeghen, Mark, Oak.	233	1012	4.3	21	3
Armstrong, Otis, Den.	247	1008	4.1	31	5

	Att	Yards	Avg	Long	TDs
Pruitt, Greg, Clev.	209	1000	4.8	64	4
Cunningham, Sam, N.E.	172	824	4.8	24	3
Young, Rickey, S.D.	162	802	5.0	t46	4
Malone, Benny, Mia.	186	797	4.3	31	4
Gaines, Clark, N.Y.J.	157	724	4.6	33	3
Calhoun, Don, N.E.	129	721	5.6	54	1
Johnson, Andy, N.E.	169	699	4.1	t69	6
Coleman, Ronnie, Hou.	171	684	4.0	39	2
Clark, Boobie, Cin.	151	671	4.4	24	7
Griffin, Archie, Cin.	138	625	4.5	t77	3
Miller, Cleo, Clev.	153	613	4.0	21	4
Willis, Fred, Hou.	148	542	3.7	44	2
Lane, MacArthur, K.C.	162	542	3.3	20	5
Bulaich, Norm, Mia.	122	540	4.4	35	4

NFC — INDIVIDUALS

	Att	Yards	Avg	Long	TDs
Payton, Walter, Chi.	311	1390	4.5	60	13
Williams, Delvin, S.F.	248	1203	4.9	t80	7
McCutcheon, Lawrence, L.A.	291	1168	4.0	40	9
Foreman, Chuck, Minn.	278	1155	4.2	46	13
Thomas, Mike, Wash.	254	1101	4.3	28	5
Otis, Jim, St. L.	233	891	3.8	23	2
Bussey, Dexter, Det.	196	858	4.4	46	3
Jackson, Wilbur, S.F.	200	792	4.0	24	1
Kotar, Doug, N.Y.G.	185	731	4.0	24	3
Cappelletti, John, L.A.	177	688	3.9	38	1
Muncie, Chuck, N.O.	149	659	4.4	51	2
Gaines, Lawrence, Det.	155	659	4.3	t26	4
Harper, Roland, Chi.	147	625	4.3	28	2
Riggins, John, Wash.	162	572	3.5	15	3
Galbreath, Tony, N.O.	136	570	4.2	t74	7
Csonka, Larry, N.Y.G.	160	569	3.6	13	4
Hogan, Mike, Phil.	123	561	4.6	32	0
Dennison, Doug, Dall.	153	542	3.5	14	6
Smith, Sherman, Sea.	119	537	4.5	t53	4
Metcalf, Terry, St. L.	134	537	4.0	36	3

AFC - TEAM

	Att	Yards	Avg	Long	TDs
Pittsburgh	653	2,971	4.5	t63	33
New England	591	2,948	5.0	t69	24
Buffalo	548	2,566	4.7	t75	11
Baltimore	565	2,303	4.1	t69	26
Cleveland	533	2,295	4.3	64	9
Oakland	557	2,285	4.1	31	14
Miami	491	2,118	4.3	t59	15
Cincinnati	481	2,109	4.4	t77	15
San Diego	473	2,040	4.3	t46	13
Denver	500	1,932	3.9	31	14
New York Jets	438	1,924	4.4	60	10
Kansas City	498	1,873	3.8	t59	18
Tampa Bay	433	1,503	3.5	46	5
Houston	416	1,498	3.6	44	6
Conference Total	7,177	30,365	—	t77	213
Conference Average	512.6	2,168.9	4.2	—	15.2

NFC - TEAM

	Att	Yards	Avg	Long	TDs
Los Angeles	613	2,528	4.1	40	23
San Francisco	576	2,447	4.2	t80	14
Chicago	578	2,363	4.1	60	20
St. Louis	580	2,301	4.0	36	17
Detroit	516	2,213	4.3	46	9
Dallas	538	2,147	4.0	28	16
Washington	548	2,111	3.9	28	10
Philadelphia	505	2,080	4.1	59	8
Minnesota	540	2,003	3.7	46	18
New York Giants	530	1,904	3.6	29	11
New Orleans	431	1,775	4.1	t74	16
Green Bay	485	1,722	3.6	56	15
Atlanta	470	1,689	3.6	47	10
Seattle	374	1,416	3.8	t53	14
Conference Total	7,284	28,699	—	t80	201
Conference Average	520.3	2,049.9	3.9	—	14.4

PASSING

INDIVIDUAL CHAMPION
AFC: 103.7 (Rating Points) Ken Stabler, Oakland
NFC: 89.8 (Rating Points) James Harris, Los Angeles

ATTEMPTS
AFC: 359 Dan Fouts, San Diego
NFC: 439 Jim Zorn, Seattle

COMPLETIONS
AFC: 208 Dan Fouts, San Diego
NFC: 255 Fran Tarkenton, Minnesota

YARDAGE
AFC: 3,104 Bert Jones, Baltimore
NFC: 2,961 Fran Tarkenton, Minnesota

TOUCHDOWN PASSES
AFC: 27 Ken Stabler, Oakland
NFC: 18 Jim Hart, St. Louis

MOST INTERCEPTIONS
AFC: 20 Steve Grogan, New England
NFC: 27 Jim Zorn, Seattle

LOWEST PERCENTAGE, PASSES HAD INTERCEPTED
AFC: 0.7 Joe Ferguson, Buffalo (1 Interception; 151
Attempts), a new NFL record
NFC: 1.9 Fran Tarkenton, Minnesota (8 Interceptions;
412 Attempts)

TEAM CHAMPION
AFC: 102.1 (Rating Points) Oakland
NFC: 85.5 (Rating Points) Minnesota

TOP TEN INDIVIDUAL QUALIFIERS

	Att	Comp	Pct Comp	Yards	Int	Rating Points
Stabler, Ken, Oak.	291	194	66.7	2737	17	103.7
Jones, Bert, Balt.	343	207	60.3	3104	9	102.6
Ferguson, Joe, Buff.	151	74	49.0	1086	1	90.0
Harris, James, L.A.	158	91	57.6	1460	6	89.8
Landry, Greg, Det.	291	168	57.7	2191	8	89.6
Tarkenton, Fran, Minn. ..	412	255	61.9	2961	8	89.4
Hart, Jim, St. L.	388	218	56.2	2946	13	81.7
Staubach, Roger, Dall. ..	369	208	56.4	2715	11	79.9
Griese, Bob, Mia	272	162	59.6	2097	12	78.9
Livingston, Mike, K.C. ..	338	189	55.9	2682	13	77.9

AFC INDIVIDUAL QUALIFIERS

	Att	Comp	Pct Comp	Yards	Int	Rating Points
Stabler, Ken, Oak.	291	194	66.7	2737	17	103.7
Jones, Bert, Balt.	343	207	60.3	3104	9	102.6
Ferguson, Joe, Buff.	151	74	49.0	1086	1	90.0
Griese, Bob, Mia.	272	162	59.6	2097	12	78.9
Livingston, Mike, K.C. ..	338	189	55.9	2682	13	77.9
Sipe, Brian, Clev.	312	178	57.1	2113	14	77.1
Anderson, Ken, Cin.	338	179	53.0	2367	14	77.0
Fouts, Dan, S.D.	359	208	57.9	2535	15	75.3
Pastorini, Dan, Hou.	309	167	54.0	1795	10	68.6
Bradshaw, Terry, Pitt. ..	192	92	47.9	1177	9	65.3
Ramsey, Steve, Den. ...	270	128	47.4	1931	13	65.1
Grogan, Steve, N.E.	302	145	48.0	1903	20	60.8
Spurrier, Steve, T.B. ...	311	156	50.2	1628	12	57.1
Namath, Joe, N.Y.J. ...	230	114	49.6	1090	16	39.7
Todd, Richard, N.Y.J. ..	162	65	40.1	870	12	33.4
Marangi, Gary, Buff.	232	82	35.3	998	16	30.7

NFC INDIVIDUAL QUALIFIERS

	Att	Comp	Pct Comp	Yards	Int	Rating Points
Harris, James, L.A.	158	91	57.6	1460	6	89.8
Landry, Greg, Det.	291	168	57.7	2191	8	89.6
Tarkenton, Fran, Minn.	412	255	61.9	2961	8	89.4
Hart, Jim, St. L.	388	218	56.2	2946	13	81.7
Staubach, Roger, Dall.	369	208	56.4	2715	11	79.9
Kilmer, Billy, Wash.	206	108	52.4	1252	10	70.0
Scott, Bobby, N.O.	190	103	54.2	1065	6	64.3
Plunkett, Jim, S.F.	243	126	51.9	1592	16	62.8
Theismann, Joe, Wash.	163	79	48.5	1036	10	59.9
Douglass, Bobby, N.O.	213	103	48.4	1288	8	58.1
Morton, Craig, N.Y.G.	284	153	53.9	1865	20	55.9
Boryla, Mike, Phil.	246	123	50.0	1247	14	53.5
Dickey, Lynn, G.B.	243	115	47.3	1465	14	52.1
Avellini, Bob, Chi.	271	118	43.5	1580	15	49.7
Zorn, Jim, Sea.	439	208	47.4	2571	27	49.2

PASS RECEIVING

INDIVIDUAL CHAMPION
AFC: 66 MacArthur Lane, Kansas City
NFC: 58 Drew Pearson, Dallas

YARDAGE
AFC: 1,112 Roger Carr, Baltimore
NFC: 906 Sammie White, Minnesota

AVERAGE GAIN
AFC: 25.9 (Yards) Roger Carr, Baltimore (43 Receptions; 1,112 Yards)
NFC: 22.9 (Yards) Ron Jessie, Los Angeles (34 Receptions; 779 Yards)

TOUCHDOWNS
AFC: 12 Cliff Branch, Oakland
NFC: 10 Sammie White, Minnesota

LONGEST
AFC: 88 (Yards) Cliff Branch, Oakland vs Green Bay, October 24 (from Ken Stabler, TD)
NFC: 85 (Yards) Delvin Williams, San Francisco vs Washington, November 7 (from Jim Plunkett, TD)

ONE GAME PERFORMANCE
AFC: 12
Dave Casper, Oakland vs New England, October 3 (136 Yards)
Lydell Mitchell, Baltimore vs New York Jets, November 28 (64 Yards)

NFC: 11
Doug Kotar, New York Giants vs St. Louis, October 3 (132 Yards)
Frank Grant, Washington vs San Francisco, November 7 (200 Yards)

TEAM LEADERS
AFC:
BALTIMORE 60 Lydell Mitchell; BUFFALO 61 Bob Chandler; CINCINNATI 41 Isaac Curtis; CLEVELAND 49 Reggie Rucker; DENVER 39 Otis Armstrong; HOUSTON 51 Ken Burrough; KANSAS CITY 66 MacArthur Lane; MIAMI 33 Nat Moore; NEW ENGLAND 29 Andy Johnson; NEW YORK JETS 41 Clark Gaines; OAKLAND 53 Dave Casper; PITTSBURGH 28 Lynn Swann; SAN DIEGO 50 Charlie Joiner; TAMPA BAY 30 Morris Owens.

NFC:
ATLANTA 41 Alfred Jenkins; CHICAGO 29 Roland Harper; DALLAS 58 Drew Pearson; DETROIT 39 Ray Jarvis; GREEN BAY 33 Ken Payne; LOS ANGELES 39 Harold Jackson; MINNESOTA 55 Chuck Foreman; NEW ORLEANS 54 Tony Galbreath; NEW YORK GIANTS 42 Bob Tucker; PHILADELPHIA 42 Harold Carmichael; ST. LOUIS 52 Ike Harris; SAN FRANCISCO 33 Wilbur Jackson & Gene Washington; SEATTLE 54 Steve Largent; WASHINGTON 50 Frank Grant.

97

TOP PASS RECEIVERS

	No	Yards	Avg	Long	TDs
Lane, MacArthur, K.C.	66	686	10.4	44	1
Chandler, Bob, Buff	61	824	13.5	t58	10
Mitchell, Lydell, Balt.	60	555	9.3	t40	3
Pearson, Drew, Dall.	58	806	13.9	t40	6
Foreman, Chuck, Minn.	55	567	10.3	t41	1
Largent, Steve, Sea.	54	705	13.1	45	4
Galbreath, Tony, N.O.	54	420	7.8	35	1
Casper, Dave, Oak.	53	691	13.0	t30	10
Rashad, Ahmad, Minn.	53	671	12.7	47	3
Harris, Ike, St. L.	52	782	15.0	40	1

AFC—INDIVIDUALS

	No	Yards	Avg	Long	TDs
Lane, MacArthur, K.C.	66	686	10.4	44	1
Chandler, Bob, Buff.	61	824	13.5	t58	10
Mitchell, Lydell, Balt.	60	555	9.3	t40	3
Casper, Dave, Oak.	53	691	13.0	t30	10
Burrough, Ken, Hou.	51	932	18.3	t69	7
Joiner, Charlie, S.D.	50	1056	21.1	t81	7
Rucker, Reggie, Clev.	49	676	13.8	45	8
White, Walter, K.C.	47	808	17.2	41	7
Johnson, Billy, Hou.	47	495	10.5	t40	4
Young, Rickey, S.D.	47	441	9.4	33	1
Branch, Cliff, Oak.	46	1111	24.2	t88	12
Pruitt, Greg, Clev.	45	341	7.6	27	1
Carr, Roger, Balt.	43	1112	25.9	t79	11
Biletnikoff, Fred, Oak.	43	551	12.8	t32	7
Curtis, Isaac, Cin.	41	766	18.7	t85	6
Gaines, Clark, N.Y.J.	41	400	9.8	27	2
Doughty, Glenn, Balt.	40	628	15.7	41	5
Coleman, Ronnie, Hou.	40	247	6.2	19	3
Armstrong, Otis, Den.	39	457	11.7	t36	1
Warfield, Paul, Clev.	38	613	16.1	t37	6

	No	Yards	Avg	Long	TDS
Pearson, Drew, Dall.	58	806	13.9	t40	6
Foreman, Chuck, Minn.	55	567	10.3	t41	1
Largent, Steve, Sea.	54	705	13.1	45	4
Galbreath, Tony, N.O.	54	420	7.8	35	1
Rashad, Ahmad, Minn.	53	671	12.7	47	3
Harris, Ike, St. L.	52	782	15.0	40	1
White, Sammie, Minn.	51	906	17.8	t56	10
Grant, Frank, Wash.	50	818	16.4	t53	5
DuPree, Billy Joe, Dall.	42	680	16.2	t38	2
Carmichael, Harold, Phil.	42	503	12.0	24	5
Tucker, Bob, N.Y.G.	42	498	11.9	39	1
Jenkins, Alfred, Atl.	41	710	17.3	t34	6
McClanahan, Brent, Minn.	40	252	6.3	23	1
Jarvis, Ray, Det.	39	822	21.1	t74	5
Jackson, Harold, L.A.	39	751	19.3	t65	5
Laidlaw, Scott, Dall.	38	325	8.6	26	1
Howard, Ron, Sea.	37	422	11.4	30	0
Gray, Mel, St. L.	36	686	19.1	t77	5
Smith, Sherman, Sea.	36	384	10.7	34	1
Kotar, Doug, N.Y.G.	36	319	8.9	30	0

INTERCEPTIONS

INDIVIDUAL CHAMPION
AFC:	9	Ken Riley, Cincinnati
NFC:	10	Monte Jackson, Los Angeles

YARDAGE
AFC:	182	Prentice McCray, New England
NFC:	206	Levi Johnson, Detroit

TOUCHDOWNS
AFC:	2	Tom Casanova, Cincinnati
		Prentice McCray, New England
		John Rowser, Denver
NFC:	3	Monte Jackson, Los Angeles

LONGEST
AFC: 101   Tony Greene, Buffalo vs Kansas City, October 3 (TD)
NFC: 83   Jim Merlo, New Orleans vs Atlanta, October 10 (TD)

TEAM LEADERS
AFC:
BALTIMORE 5 Jackie Wallace; BUFFALO 5 Tony Greene; CINCINNATI 9 Ken Riley; CLEVELAND 7 Thom Darden; DENVER 7 Tom Jackson; HOUSTON 5 C. L. Whittington; KANSAS CITY 5 Kerry Reardon; MIAMI 2 Charlie Babb, Ken Ellis, Bob Matheson & Jeris White; NEW ENGLAND 8 Mike Haynes; NEW YORK JETS 2 Greg Buttle, Bob Martin, Rich Sowells & Ed Taylor; OAKLAND 4 Monte Johnson; PITTSBURGH 6 Mel Blount & Glen Edwards; SAN DIEGO 6 Don Goode; TAMPA BAY 3 Mark Cotney

NFC:
ATLANTA 6 Rolland Lawrence; CHICAGO 7 Ross Brupbacher; DALLAS 4 Mark Washington; DETROIT 7 James Hunter; GREEN BAY 4 Johnnie Gray; LOS ANGELES 10 Monte Jackson; MINNESOTA 7 Nate Wright; NEW ORLEANS 4 Jim Merlo; NEW YORK GIANTS 2 Jim Stienke, Brad Van Pelt & Rick Volk; PHILADELPHIA 2 Bill Bergey, Bill Bradley & John Outlaw; ST. LOUIS 4 Mike Sensibaugh, Norm Thompson & Roger Wehrli; SAN FRANCISCO 3 Bruce Rhodes; SEATTLE 4 Dave Brown & Rolly Woolsey; WASHINGTON 8 Joe Lavender

TEAM CHAMPION
AFC: 26   Cincinnati
NFC: 32   Los Angeles

TOP TEN INTERCEPTORS

	No	Yards	Avg	Long	TDs
Jackson, Monte, L.A.	10	173	17.3	t46	3
Riley, Ken, Cin.	9	141	15.7	t53	1
Haynes, Mike, N.E.	8	90	11.3	28	0
Perry, Rod, L.A.	8	79	9.9	43	0
Lavender, Joe, Wash.	8	77	9.6	28	0
Jackson, Tom, Den.	7	136	19.4	t46	1
Hunter, James, Det.	7	120	17.1	t39	1
Darden, Thom, Clev.	7	73	10.4	21	0

	No	Yards	Avg	Long	TDs
Brupbacher, Ross, Chi.	7	49	7.0	25	0
Wright, Nate, Minn.	7	47	6.7	21	0

AFC—INDIVIDUALS

	No	Yards	Avg	Long	TDs
Riley, Ken, Cin.	9	141	15.7	t53	1
Haynes, Mike, N.E.	8	90	11.3	28	0
Jackson, Tom, Den.	7	136	19.4	t46	1
Darden, Thom, Clev.	7	73	10.4	21	0
Edwards, Glen, Pitt.	6	95	15.8	55	0
Goode, Don, S.D.	6	82	13.7	27	0
Blount, Mel, Pitt.	6	75	12.5	28	0
McCray, Prentice, N.E.	5	182	36.4	t63	2
Greene, Tony, Buff.	5	135	27.0	t101	1
Casanova, Tom, Cin.	5	109	21.8	t33	2
Wallace, Jackie, Balt.	5	105	21.0	41	0
Whittington, C. L., Hou.	5	103	20.6	50	0
Reardon, Kerry, K. C.	5	26	5.2	22	0
Rowser, John, Den.	4	104	26.0	t41	2
Foley, Steve, Den.	4	95	23.8	34	0
Williams, Mike, S.D.	4	76	19.0	35	0
Johnson, Monte, Oak.	4	40	10.0	22	0
Gray, Tim, K.C.	4	19	4.8	11	0
Scott, Clarence, Clev.	4	11	2.8	5	0
Bolton, Ron, Clev.	3	76	25.3	39	1

NFC—INDIVIDUALS

	No	Yards	Avg	Long	TDs
Jackson, Monte, L.A.	10	173	17.3	t46	3
Perry, Rod, L.A.	8	79	9.9	43	0
Lavender, Joe, Wash.	8	77	9.6	28	0
Hunter, James, Det.	7	120	17.1	t39	1
Brupbacher, Ross, Chi.	7	49	7.0	25	0
Wright, Nate, Minn.	7	47	6.7	21	0
Johnson, Levi, Det.	6	206	34.3	76	1
Ellis, Allan, Chi.	6	47	7.8	t22	1

	No	Yards	Avg	Long	TDs
Lawrence, Rolland, Atl.	6	43	7.2	22	0
Fischer, Pat, Wash.	5	38	7.6	32	0
Merlo, Jim, N.O.	4	142	35.5	t83	2
Gray, Johnnie, G.B.	4	101	25.3	67	1
Thompson, Norm, St. L.	4	83	20.8	38	0
Brown, Dave, Sea.	4	70	17.5	33	0
Simpson, Bill, L.A.	4	62	15.5	30	0
Sensibaugh, Mike, St. L.	4	60	15.0	t35	1
Washington, Mark, Dall.	4	49	12.3	22	0
Plank, Doug, Chi.	4	31	7.8	15	0
Wehrli, Roger, St. L.	4	31	7.8	26	0
Robertson, Isiah, L.A.	4	28	7.0	14	0

PUNTING

INDIVIDUAL CHAMPION
AFC: 42.8 (Yard Average) Marv Bateman, Buffalo (86 Punts; 3,678 Yards)

NFC: 42.1 (Yard Average) John James, Atlanta (101 Punts; 4,253 Yards)

NET AVERAGE
AFC: 34.8 David Lee, Baltimore (59 Total Punts; 2,051 Net Yards)

NFC: 36.2 John James, Atlanta (101 Total Punts; 3,653 Net Yards)

LONGEST
AFC: 78 (Yards) Marv Bateman, Buffalo vs Houston, September 19

NFC: 69 (Yards) Herman Weaver, Detroit vs Chicago, September 12

MOST
AFC: 92 Dave Green, Tampa Bay (0 Blocked)

NFC: 101 Tom Blanchard, New Orleans (0 Blocked)
John James, Atlanta (0 Blocked)

TEAM CHAMPION

AFC: 42.3 (Yard Average) Buffalo
NFC: 42.1 (Yard Average) Atlanta

TOP TEN PUNTERS

	Punts	Yards	Long	Avg	Blk
Bateman, Marv, Buff.	86	3678	78	42.8	1
James, John, Atl.	101	4253	67	42.1	0
Wilson, Jerrel, K.C.	65	2729	62	42.0	1
Guy, Ray, Oak.	67	2785	66	41.6	0
Jennings, Dave, N.Y.G.	74	3054	61	41.3	3
Wittum, Tom, S.F.	89	3634	68	40.8	2
West, Jeff, S.D.	38	1548	57	40.7	0
Patrick, Mike, N.E.	67	2688	52	40.1	0
Carrell, Duane, N.Y.J.	81	3218	72	39.7	0
Lee, David, Balt.	59	2342	56	39.7	0

AFC - INDIVIDUALS

	Punts	Yards	Long	Avg	Blk
Bateman, Marv, Buff.	86	3678	78	42.8	1
Wilson, Jerrel, K.C.	65	2729	62	42.0	1
Guy, Ray, Oak.	67	2785	66	41.6	0
West, Jeff, S.D.	38	1548	57	40.7	0
Patrick, Mike, N.E.	67	2688	52	40.1	0
Carrell, Duane, N.Y.J.	81	3218	72	39.7	0
Lee, David, Balt.	59	2342	56	39.7	0
McInally, Pat, Cin.	76	2999	61	39.5	0
Green, Dave, T.B.	92	3619	56	39.3	0
Walden, Bobby, Pitt.	76	2982	58	39.2	0
Cockroft, Don, Clev.	64	2487	51	38.9	3
Seiple, Larry, Mia.	62	2366	56	38.2	0
Hoopes, Mitch, S.D.-Hou.	49	1849	57	37.7	2
Pastorini, Dan, Hou.	70	2571	74	36.7	0
Weese, Norris, Den.	52	1852	55	35.6	0

NFC - INDIVIDUALS

	Punts	Yards	Long	Avg	Blk
James, John, Atl.	101	4253	67	42.1	0
Jennings, Dave, N.Y.G.	74	3054	61	41.3	3
Wittum, Tom, S.F.	89	3634	68	40.8	2
Weaver, Herman, Det.	83	3280	69	39.5	1
Blanchard, Tom, N.O.	101	3974	63	39.3	0
Jackson, Rusty, L.A.	77	3006	61	39.0	2
Bragg, Mike, Wash.	90	3503	56	38.9	0
Clabo, Neil, Minn.	69	2678	55	38.8	0
White, Danny, Dall.	70	2690	54	38.4	2
Engles, Rich, Sea.	80	3067	55	38.3	2
Parsons, Bob, Chi.	99	3726	62	37.6	1
Beverly, David, G.B.	83	3074	60	37.0	1
Jones, Spike, Phil.	94	3445	57	36.6	3
Joyce, Terry, St.L.	64	2331	54	36.4	2

PUNT RETURNS

INDIVIDUAL CHAMPION
AFC: 13.7 (Yard Average) Rick Upchurch, Denver (39 Returns; 536 Yards)
NFC: 13.5 (Yard Average) Eddie Brown, Washington (48 Returns; 646 Yards)

YARDAGE
AFC: 608 Mike Haynes, New England
NFC: 646 Eddie Brown, Washington

RETURNS
AFC: 45 Mike Haynes, New England
NFC: 54 Rolland Lawrence, Atlanta, new NFL record

LONGEST
AFC: 92 (Yards) Rick Upchurch, Denver vs San Diego, October 3 (TD)
NFC: 71 (Yards) Eddie Brown, Washington vs St. Louis, October 25 (TD)

TOUCHDOWNS

AFC: 10 Rick Upchurch, Denver (4) vs Cleveland, September 26 (73 & 47 Yards), vs San Diego, October 3 (92 Yards), vs Kansas City, October 24 (55 Yards); Mike Haynes, New England (2) vs Buffalo, November 7 (89 Yards), vs Denver, November 28 (62 Yards); Ron Coleman, Houston vs Cincinnati, October 24 (69 Yards); Keith Moody, Buffalo vs New York Jets, October 10 (67 Yards); Lou Piccone, New York Jets vs Tampa Bay, November 14 (60 Yards); Freddie Solomon, Miami vs Buffalo, December 5 (79 Yards)

NFC: 3 Eddie Brown, Washington vs St. Louis, October 25 (71 Yards); Anthony Leonard, San Francisco vs New Orleans, October 17 (60 Yards); Ralph McGill, San Francisco vs Seattle, September 26 (50 Yards)

TEAM CHAMPION

AFC: 13.1 (Yard Average) New England (48 Returns; 628 Yards)
NFC: 13.2 (Yard Average) Washington (52 Returns; 688 Yards)

TOP TEN PUNT RETURNERS

	No	FC	Yards	Avg	Long	TDs
Upchurch, Rick, Den.	39	3	536	13.7	t92	4
Haynes, Mike, N.E.	45	0	608	13.5	t89	2
Brown, Eddie, Wash.	48	8	646	13.5	t71	1
Fuller, Mike, S.D.	33	0	436	13.2	43	0
Brunson, Larry, K.C.	31	0	387	12.5	48	0
Bryant, Cullen, L.A.	29	2	321	11.1	25	0
Metcalf, Terry, St.L.	17	1	188	11.1	39	0
Colzie, Neal, Oak.	41	3	448	10.9	32	0
Johnson, Butch, Dall.	45	11	489	10.9	55	0
Marshall, Larry, Phil.	27	9	290	10.7	29	0

AFC - INDIVIDUALS

	No	FC	Yards	Avg	Long	TDs
Upchurch, Rick, Den.	39	3	536	13.7	t92	4
Haynes, Mike, N.E.	45	0	608	13.5	t89	2
Fuller, Mike, S.D.	33	0	436	13.2	43	0
Brunson, Larry, K.C.	31	0	387	12.5	48	0
Colzie, Neal, Oak.	41	3	448	10.9	32	0

	No	FC	Yards	Avg	Long	TDs
Johnson, Billy, Hou.	38	9	403	10.6	46	0
Moody, Keith, Buff.	16	8	166	10.4	t67	1
Bell, Theo, Pitt.	39	2	390	10.0	35	0
Moore, Manfred, T.B.-Oak. . . .	20	0	184	9.2	23	0
Deloplaine, Jack, Pitt.	17	0	150	8.8	36	0
Piccone, Lou, N.Y.J.	21	0	173	8.2	t60	1
Stevens, Howard, Balt.	39	9	315	8.1	44	0
Shelby, Willie, Cin.	21	4	162	7.7	30	0
Reece, Danny, T.B.	20	0	143	7.2	30	0
Holden, Steve, Clev.	31	2	205	6.6	38	0
Parrish, Lemar, Cin.	20	2	122	6.1	32	0

NFC - INDIVIDUALS

	No	FC	Yards	Avg	Long	TDs
Brown, Eddie, Wash.	48	8	646	13.5	t71	1
Bryant, Cullen, L.A.	29	2	321	11.1	25	0
Metcalf, Terry, St. L.	17	1	188	11.1	39	0
Johnson, Butch, Dall.	45	11	489	10.9	55	0
Marshall, Larry, Phil.	27	9	290	10.7	29	0
Tilley, Pat, St. L.	15	0	146	9.7	17	0
Athas, Pete, N.O.	35	10	332	9.5	67	0
Rhodes, Bruce, S.F.	16	2	142	8.9	22	0
Leonard, Anthony, S.F.	35	5	293	8.4	t60	1
Barney, Lem, Det.	23	22	191	8.3	30	0
Gray, Johnnie, G.B.	37	7	307	8.3	27	0
Livers, Virgil, Chi.	28	0	205	7.3	51	0
Blackwood, Lyle, Sea.	19	2	132	6.9	26	0
Willis, Leonard, Minn.	30	10	207	6.9	29	0
Lawrence, Rolland, Atl.	54	5	372	6.9	24	0
Robinson, Jim, N.Y.G.	24	7	106	4.4	22	0

KICKOFF RETURNS

INDIVIDUAL CHAMPION

AFC: 32.9 (Yard Average) Duriel Harris, Miami (17 Returns;
   559 Yards)

NFC: 28.7 (Yard Average) Cullen Bryant, Los Angeles (16 returns;
   459 Yards)

YARDAGE

AFC: 761 Willie Shelby, Cincinnati
NFC: 754 Brian Baschnagel, Chicago

RETURNS

AFC: 31 Lou Piccone, New York Jets
NFC: 30 Eddie Brown, Washington
Larry Marshall, Philadelphia
Oliver Ross, Seattle

LONGEST

AFC: 97 (Yards) Willie Shelby, Cincinnati vs Cleveland,
October 3 (TD)
NFC: 90 (Yards) Cullen Bryant, Los Angeles vs St. Louis,
November 14 (TD)

TOUCHDOWNS

AFC: 1 Willie Shelby, Cincinnati vs Cleveland, October 3 (97 Yards)
NFC: 1 Cullen Bryant, Los Angeles vs St. Louis, November 14
(90 Yards)

TEAM CHAMPION

AFC: 24.5 (Yard Average) Miami (55 Returns; 1,347 Yards)
NFC: 24.5 (Yard Average) Dallas (42 Returns, 1,027 Yards)

TOP TEN KICKOFF RETURNERS

	No	Yards	Avg	Long	TDs
Harris, Duriel, Mia.	17	559	32.9	69	0
Bryant, Cullen, L.A.	16	459	28.7	t90	1
Phillips, Jess, N.E.	14	397	28.4	71	0
Perrin, Lonnie, Den.	14	391	27.9	43	0
Williams, Lawrence, K.C.	25	688	27.5	64	0
Hunter, James, Det.	14	375	26.8	84	0
Jennings, Rick, Oak.	16	417	26.1	55	0
Baschnagel, Brian, Chi.	29	754	26.0	48	0
McCoy, Mike C., G.B.	18	457	25.4	65	0
Shelby, Willie, Cin.	30	761	25.4	t97	1

AFC - INDIVIDUALS

	No	Yards	Avg	Long	TDs
Harris, Duriel, Mia.	17	559	32.9	69	0
Phillips, Jess, N.E.	14	397	28.4	71	0

	No	Yards	Avg	Long	TDs
Perrin, Lonnie, Den.	14	391	27.9	43	0
Williams, Lawrence, K.C.	25	688	27.5	64	0
Jennings, Rick, Oak.	16	417	26.1	55	0
Shelby, Willie, Cin.	30	761	25.4	t97	1
Holden, Steve, Clev.	19	461	24.3	44	0
Davis, Gary, Mia.	26	617	23.7	47	0
Stevens, Howard, Balt.	30	710	23.7	83	0
Upchurch, Rick, Den.	22	514	23.4	64	0
Moody, Keith, Buff.	26	605	23.3	41	0
Feacher, Ricky, N.E.-Clev.	24	551	23.0	46	0
Giammona, Louie, N.Y.J.	23	527	22.9	34	0
Hooks, Roland, Buff.	23	521	22.7	79	0
Deloplaine, Jack, Pitt.	17	385	22.6	39	0
McNeil, Rod, T.B.	17	384	22.6	43	0
Piccone, Lou, N.Y.J.	31	699	22.5	58	0
Reamon, Tommy, K.C.	19	424	22.3	35	0
Johnson, Billy, Hou.	26	579	22.3	53	0
Owens, Art. S.D.	25	551	22.0	40	0

NFC - INDIVIDUALS

	No	Yards	Avg	Long	TDs
Bryant, Cullen, L.A.	16	459	28.7	t90	1
Hunter, James, Det.	14	375	26.8	84	0
Baschnagel, Brian, Chi.	29	754	26.0	48	0
McCoy, Mike C., G.B.	18	457	25.4	65	0
Lawrence, Rolland, Atl.	21	521	24.8	36	0
Johnson, Butch, Dall.	28	693	24.8	74	0
Brown, Eddie, Wash.	30	738	24.6	67	0
Willis, Leonard, Minn.	24	552	23.0	57	0
Latin, Jerry, St. L.	16	357	22.3	39	0
Robinson, Jim, N.Y.G.	20	444	22.2	32	0
Ross, Oliver, Sea.	30	655	21.8	45	0
Marshall, Larry, Phil.	30	651	21.7	41	0
Leonard, Anthony, S.F.	26	553	21.3	39	0
Odom, Steve, G.B.	29	610	21.0	88	0
Metcalf, Terry, St. L.	16	325	20.3	33	0
Galbreath, Tony, N.O.	20	399	20.0	32	0